# Reading Tutor:
# Weird, But True

By
## CINDY BARDEN

COPYRIGHT © 2004 Mark Twain Media, Inc.

ISBN 1-58037-262-7

Printing No. CD-1622

Mark Twain Media, Inc., Publishers
Distributed by Carson-Dellosa Publishing Company, Inc.

# Table of Contents

# Introduction

Students of all reading abilities require interesting and readable material, particularly reluctant readers who may struggle in the classroom. The Reading Tutor series engages the interests of these students through individualized tutoring in highly readable, age-appropriate activities. The series introduces and strengthens concepts needed to build and reinforce reading skills for students in grades four through eight.

The Reading Tutor series comprises an array of titles with high-interest topics, including animals, sports, inventions, biographies, and weird, but true facts.

Designed in a lively, non-intimidating format, the reproducible activities include games, stories, riddles, puzzles, and other stimulating materials to improve reading skills and broaden reading interests, which will enrich the reading experience for the struggling learner.

The activities in the Reading Tutor series focus on a variety of concepts and skills, including grammar basics, using the Internet and other types of reference sources, sequencing, comparing and contrasting, finding the main idea, differentiating between facts and opinions, and using context clues to expand vocabulary.

A sidebar on each page clearly states the concept or skill reinforced by that activity. This format allows students to master one concept or skill at a time, thereby building confidence and proficiency.

Tutors can tailor the reading program for specific students in two ways: by selecting the books in this series that include topics of particular interest to an individual student and by selecting specific activities that will reinforce the skills that student needs most.

To provide additional reinforcement, suggestions for further reading offer an opportunity to lead students to seek out more information on subjects that interest them.

Name: _____  Date: _____

# Motorcycles Aren't What They Used to Be

When you **compare** two items, you look for ways in which they are alike.

To **contrast** means to list ways in which the items are different.

**Directions:** Read about early motorcycles, and then complete the chart.

In 1885, Gottlieb Daimler of Germany built the first motorcycle by attaching a small gasoline engine to a wooden bicycle frame. The wooden wheels came from a horse-drawn carriage. He used a leather horse saddle for the seat.

Early motorcycles had pedals like bikes. The engines weren't strong enough to ride up hills, so riders had to pedal. The engines weren't very reliable either. They often broke down. Riders had to carry gasoline with them because there were no gas stations.

Fortunately, if the engine didn't work or the motorcycle ran out of gas, the rider could always keep pedaling.

Can you imagine a group of Harley™ riders pedaling down the highway today?

|                | Early Motorcycles | Motorcycles Today |
|----------------|-------------------|-------------------|
| wheels         |                   |                   |
| frame          |                   |                   |
| seat           |                   |                   |
| engine         |                   |                   |
| advantages     |                   |                   |
| disadvantages  |                   |                   |

Name: _____ Date: _____

# The Cold Shoulder

A **noun** is the name of a person, place, thing, or idea. *King, castle, sheep,* and *respect* are nouns.

A **personal pronoun** takes the place of a noun. Personal pronouns include *I, he, she, we, it, they, them, us,* and *you.*

**Directions:** Underline all the nouns and personal pronouns in the article.

1. Have you ever heard the expression, "to give someone the cold shoulder"?

2. It means to ignore someone or to treat that person with very little respect.

3. The expression probably began hundreds of years ago in England.

4. When an important guest like a knight arrived at a castle, people treated him with respect and honor.

5. His host provided the best meat and drink.

6. Others who came to a castle didn't get treated as well.

7. They might get only water and a plate of cold meat, often mutton.

8. The shoulder was one of the toughest parts of the meat.

9. Visitors who were not important might receive only a piece of cold shoulder.

10. When you ignore a classmate or exclude someone from a game or activity, you treat that person with disrespect, or "the cold shoulder."

How would you feel if someone gave you "the cold shoulder"?

_____

_____

_____

_____

Name: _____ Date: _____

# The Midnight Ride of Paul Revere

A **fact** is a true statement that can be proven.

An **opinion** is a belief someone has about an event.

Henry Wadsworth Longfellow's poem, "Paul Revere's Ride," became very popular in the 1860s. He wrote about a real event, but he changed the facts a bit. Paul Revere became the hero of the poem.

What really happened?

On the night of April 18, 1775, Paul Revere left Boston. He rode to Lexington to warn Samuel Adams and John Hancock that British soldiers planned to arrest them. He also needed to alert the Patriots in nearby Concord about a British raid.

William Dawes also set out to deliver the same warnings, but he took a different route.

On his way to Lexington, Paul Revere stopped at houses to deliver the warning: "The British are coming!" Around midnight, he gave Adams and Hancock the message, so they had time to escape.

When Dawes arrived, the two men set off for Concord. On the way, Dr. Samuel Prescott joined them.

Before they reached Concord, a British patrol arrested the three men. Dawes and Prescott escaped, but Dawes fell from his horse. He couldn't continue. The British took away Paul Revere's horse. He had to walk back to Lexington.

Only Prescott made it to Concord. His early warning helped the Patriots win the first battle of the Revolutionary War.

1. In your opinion, was Paul Revere a hero? Why or why not?

_____

_____

_____

2. Write two facts you learned about Paul Revere's ride.

_____

_____

Name: _____  Date: _____

# All Aboard for Teakettle Junction!

A **map** provides information about an area as small as a room or as large as a planet.

**Directions:** Select one of the California place names below, and write a short story on the next page that explains how that place got its name. You may research using the Internet, an atlas, the encyclopedia, and/or other resources to find out some facts about the name, or just make up your own story. (Spanish names have the English meaning in parentheses.) Next, try to locate and label the place you have selected on the California map on page 6.

| | | | |
|---|---|---|---|
| Advanal | Hellhole Palms | Shrub | Boca (Mouth) |
| Arcade | Hells Kitchen | Siberia | Bonita (Beautiful) |
| Aromas | Honda | Skidoo | Chico (Little Boy) |
| Badwater | Honeydew | Sky High | Chula Vista (Insolent |
| Bee Rock | Igo | Skytop | View) |
| Bend | Jupiter | Soapweed | Escondido (Hidden) |
| Blunt | Keg | Soda Springs | Fortuna (Fortune) |
| Bumblebee | Last Chance | Squabbletown | Los Gatos (The Cats) |
| Bummerville | Laws | Steam | Los Olivos (The Olive |
| Cabbage Patch | Little Penny | Stone | Trees) |
| Cactus | Mad River | Stovepipe | Los Osos (The Bears) |
| Clapper Gap | Mormon Bar | Strawberry | Mariposa (Butterfly) |
| Confidence | Mystic | Sucker Flat | Pajaro (Bird) |
| Cool | Needles | Surf | Palo Verde (Green |
| Cow Creek | Ono | Surfside | Wood) |
| Dairyville | Peanut | Surprise | Rancho Llano Seco (Dry |
| Deadman Crossing | Plaster City | Tarzana | Level Farm) |
| Deadwood | Priest | Teakettle Junction | Roblar (To Rivet) |
| Doghouse Junction | Ragtown | Thorn | Salinas (Salt Mines) |
| Dogtown | Rainbow | Timbuctoo | Sandia (Watermelon) |
| Fallen Leaf | Relief | Toadtown | Soledad (Solitude) |
| Freedom | Rescue | Truths Home | Tierra del Sol (Land of |
| Frying Pan | Rice | Volcano | the Sun) |
| Gas Point | Roads End | Weed | Tortuga (Turtle) |
| Globe | Rough and Ready | Weed Patch | Verde (Green) |
| Hallelujah Junction | Sargent | Wimp | |
| Hardy | Scarface | You Bet | |
| Harmony | Secret Town | Yreka Zzyzx | |

Name: _____  Date: _____

## All Aboard for Teakettle Junction (cont.)

_____

_____

_____

_____

_____

_____

_____

_____

_____

_____

_____

_____

_____

_____

_____

_____

_____

_____

Name: _____ Date: _____

# Welcome to Roachtown, Idaho

An **atlas** contains maps and information about places. It shows the names and locations of cities, states, countries, rivers, and mountains. You can find the number of people in a country or the name of an ocean.

Have you ever been to Bald Knob, Arkansas, or Monkey's Eyebrow, Kentucky?

**Directions:** Look through a United States atlas, and complete the following activity.

1.  List five types of information you found in the atlas.

    _____

    _____

    _____

    _____

    _____

2.  In the atlas, find the state in which you live. List some weird place names in your state.

    _____

    _____

    _____

    _____

3.  If you could make up a name for a new place, what would it be?

    _____

4.  Explain why you selected that name.

    _____

    _____

    _____

Name: _____     Date: _____

# Rollo, the Red-Nosed Reindeer?

You can sometimes understand the meaning of a word you don't know by using context clues.

**Context clues** are other words in the sentence or paragraph that help explain the meaning of the word.

In the 1930s, many store Santas gave children candy or small toys at Christmas. In 1939, the owners of the Montgomery Ward store in Chicago <u>decided</u> to give away something <u>unique</u>. What could their store Santa give children that would be different from the other stores' Santas?

Robert May worked for the store. He wrote a poem about a reindeer with a <u>shiny</u> nose. The reindeer <u>rescued</u> Christmas. He helped Santa find his way on a foggy Christmas Eve.

Robert May wanted to name the reindeer Rollo or Reginald; however, the store owners didn't like either name.

The <u>author</u>'s four-year-old daughter finally <u>solved</u> the problem. "Rudolph" was the right name, she <u>insisted</u>. Rudolph became the name of the most famous red-nosed reindeer.

The Montgomery Ward Santa gave each child who visited an <u>illustrated</u> copy of the poem. Children loved the pictures and the poem. The poem became a song in 1947. We know it as "Rudolph, the Red-Nosed Reindeer."

**Directions:** Fill in the blanks with underlined words from the article that match the definitions.

1. writer          __ __ __ __ __ **R**

2. fixed           __ __ __ __ **E** __

3. chose           __ __ __ **I** __ __ __

4. bright          __ __ __ **N** __

5. saved           __ __ __ __ __ __ **D**

6. demanded        __ __ __ __ __ __ **E** __

7. one of a kind   __ __ __ __ __ **E**

8. with pictures   __ __ __ __ __ __ **R** __ __ __

Name: _____ Date: _____

# That's Ridiculous!

People write **editorials** to express their opinions about something that they believe is important.

**Directions:** Select one of these weird, but true events. On your own paper, write an editorial expressing your opinion of the event.

- In 1656, Captain Kemble of Boston was sentenced to sit in the stocks for two hours because of improper behavior on a Sunday. He had kissed his wife in public after returning from a three-year sea voyage!

- Fifteen women lost their jobs at the Curtis Publishing Company in Philadelphia, Pennsylvania, in 1912 for dancing the "Turkey Trot" while on the job.

- In 1939, pinball machines were illegal in Atlanta, Georgia.

- In 1660, Massachusetts outlawed the celebration of Christmas. Offenders were fined five shillings.

- Thirty men were arrested in Connecticut in 1674 for wearing silk and having long hair.

- In 1712, people who drove their wagons recklessly in Philadelphia were fined for speeding.

- In 1925, a dog was convicted of killing a cat and sent to prison. He died of old age after spending his last six years in a prison in Philadelphia.

- In colonial times when someone was convicted of a crime and not executed, they would sometimes be branded on the base of the thumb of the right hand. From this punishment comes the custom of raising one's hand when swearing in court. The court could see if a person had been found guilty of previous crimes.

Name: _____ Date: _____

# President Fined for Speeding

A **proper noun** is the name of a specific person, place, or thing. Proper nouns are always capitalized. *George Washington, Grand Canyon,* and *Liberty Bell* are proper nouns.

**Directions:** Circle the proper nouns that should be capitalized.

1. Before he became president, ulysses s. grant was arrested twice for speeding. He paid a five-dollar fine each time—for riding his horse too fast.

2. george washington, thomas jefferson, and john adams enjoyed collecting and playing marbles, even as adults.

3. john quincy adams planted mulberry trees on the white house lawn. His wife, louisa adams, spun silk from silkworms that lived on the trees. To relax, Adams liked to go for long walks, play pool, and swim nude in the potomac river.

4. Born in a log cabin, millard fillmore didn't attend school until he was 19 years old. After attending new hope academy for six months, he fell in love with his teacher. He later married her.

5. When harry s truman ran for president, most people thought he would lose. The *Chicago Daily Tribune* announced the results on the morning after the election: DEWEY DEFEATS TRUMAN! They printed different headlines the next day. truman had won by over two million popular votes!

6. Why did abe lincoln wear a stovepipe hat? When he was a lawyer, he carried important papers in his hat.

7. The twentieth president of the united states, james garfield, was the last president to be born in a log cabin. He could also write in greek with one hand, while he wrote in latin with his other hand.

Name: _____  Date: _____

# In the White House

A **dictionary** gives the meanings and pronunciations of words. Some dictionaries list the parts of speech and origins of words.

**Did you know?** When John Quincy Adams was president, he kept a pet alligator in the East Room of the White House.

**Directions:** Read these weird, but true facts about U.S. Presidents. Use a dictionary. Write a short definition for each underlined word.

Electricity was <u>installed</u> in the White House while Benjamin Harrison was president. He and his wife feared it. They refused to touch any of the switches. Sometimes they left the lights on all night if servants weren't <u>available</u> to turn them off.

1. installed: _____

   _____

2. available: _____

   _____

President Jackson had little <u>formal</u> education as a child. He learned to read and write, but his spelling might be called "<u>creative</u>." Even as president, Jackson spelled the same word several different ways—on the same page.

3. formal: _____

4. creative: _____

Grover Cleveland <u>avoided</u> being <u>drafted</u> during the Civil War by paying a <u>substitute</u> to serve in his place.

5. avoided: _____

6. drafted: _____

7. substitute: _____

Name: _____  Date: _____

# Staying Healthy

**Directions:** Use a thesaurus. Write a synonym for each underlined word.

One hundred years ago, people did not understand the <u>importance</u> of vitamins.

1. importance: _____

Doctors and scientists <u>realized</u> that some types of food made people healthier, but the word *vitamins* wasn't used until 1911.

2. realized: _____

They also knew that the <u>absence</u> of some types of foods caused <u>disease</u>.

3. absence: _____

4. disease: _____

James Lind, a British Navy doctor, <u>verified</u> that eating fruit, especially lemons, limes, and oranges, could <u>prevent</u> a disease called scurvy.

5. verified: _____

6. prevent: _____

Sailors often suffered from scurvy during <u>extended</u> trips at sea.

7. extended: _____

In 1804, the British Navy <u>issued</u> <u>rations</u> of lemons or limes to sailors.

8. issued: _____

9. rations: _____

As a result, British sailors <u>received</u> the nickname "limey," a term still used today.

10. received: _____

Name: _____ Date: _____

# Where Did Santa Claus Come From?

**Antonyms** are words that mean the opposite. *Happy* and *sad* are antonyms. Use a dictionary or some thesauruses to find antonyms.

The idea of giving gifts at Christmas goes back to the beginning of Christianity. The shepherds and wise men brought gifts to the baby Jesus.

Thomas Nast, a cartoonist, and Clement Moore, author of "A Visit from St. Nicholas," used legends and folk tales from around the world to create the modern image of Santa Claus.

St. Nicholas actually lived in Turkey in the fourth century. According to legends, he left gifts in people's shoes or in stockings hung by the fireplace to dry.

In his poem, Moore says, "the stockings were hung by the chimney with care, in hopes that St. Nicholas soon would be there."

Stories about St. Nicholas spread to other countries. In each country, the stories changed a little bit.

From Germany came the idea of a man dressed in a red, fur-lined suit. Moore described St. Nicholas as "dressed all in fur, from his head to his foot." He carried "a bundle of toys he had flung on his back."

**Directions:** Write antonyms for these words. If you need help, use a dictionary or a thesaurus.

1.  soon: _____

2.  beginning: _____

3.  modern: _____

4.  changed: _____

5.  little: _____

6.  brought: _____

Name: _____ Date: _____

# Where Did Santa Claus Come From? (cont.)

A **simile** is a figure of speech that uses the words *like* or *as* to compare two things that are not alike.

*Example:* "Away to the window, I flew like a flash" is a simile.

Russian tales said that St. Nicholas lived at the North Pole. In Scandinavian stories, he rode in a sled pulled by magic reindeer. Legends from that area also told how he could slip down chimneys to bring gifts.

In England, people pictured him with a long white beard. They called him *Father Christmas*.

Dutch stories claimed that Santa made a list of the good and bad deeds children did during the year. The name Santa Claus came from the Dutch name, *Sinter Klaas*.

In 1881, Thomas Nast drew his version of Santa Claus to accompany Clement Moore's poem published in "Harper's Weekly." His image of Santa Claus has become an American tradition.

1. Underline the similes in these lines from Clement Moore's poem.

   "His eyes—how they twinkled, his dimples, how merry,
   His cheeks were like roses, his nose like a cherry!
   His droll little mouth was drawn up like a bow,
   And the beard of his chin was as white as the snow.
   The stump of a pipe he held tight in his teeth
   And the smoke it encircled his head like a wreath.
   He had a broad face and a little round belly,
   That shook when he laughed, like a bowlful of jelly.
   He was chubby and plump, a right jolly old elf ...

2. Write two similes of your own about Santa Claus.

   _____

   _____

   _____

   _____

Name: _____ Date: _____

# Up, Up, and Away

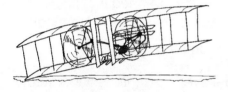

A **verb** is a word that shows action or being. *Hop, skip,* and *jump* are action verbs.

**Directions:** Underline all of the action verbs.

1. The first manned balloon flight across the English Channel took place in 1785. Dr. John Jeffries and Jean-Pierre Blanchard left England and landed in a forest in France.

2. To avoid landing in the icy waters of the English Channel, they were forced to throw out almost everything, including most of their clothing. The last item thrown overboard was Blanchard's trousers.

3. On December 17, 1903, Orville and Wilbur Wright made the first successful flight in a heavier-than-air machine. Their airplane didn't fly very far (only about 120 feet), very fast (only 30 mph), very high (only a few feet off the ground), or very long (only 12 seconds), but it did fly.

4. President Wilson planned to introduce airmail service at a special ceremony in Washington, D.C., in 1918. Thousands of spectators gathered to watch the event.

5. When the pilot couldn't get the plane started, the crowd got restless. Finally, someone discovered that the fuel tank was empty.

6. Once they fixed that problem, the pilot took off, but he went the wrong way. He made an emergency landing to get directions. That's when his propeller broke.

7. A truck finally arrived, picked up the 140 pounds of mail, and drove it to Philadelphia.

8. In 1938, Douglas Corrigan, an unemployed airplane mechanic, left Brooklyn, New York, to fly to Los Angeles. When he landed 28 hours and 13 minutes later, he found himself in Dublin, Ireland.

9. He received the nickname "Wrong Way" Corrigan because he claimed he accidentally followed the wrong end of the compass needle.

Name: _____  Date: _____

# Generally Speaking

**Zachary Taylor**

**Directions:** Use context clues to select the meaning for the underlined words and mark the correct answer.

Zachary Taylor's nickname, "Old Rough and Ready," came from the <u>battered</u> straw hat and old clothes he usually wore. The higher the rank he <u>attained</u>, the shabbier his clothes became. As a general, he wore old farm clothes. Before being elected president, Taylor never held an elected office. He had never even voted in an election.

1. <u>battered</u> means:     ○ a. old and worn out
   ○ b. fancy          ○ c. a light brown color

2. <u>attained</u> means:     ○ a. grew
   ○ b. earned        ○ c. promoted

General Ulysses S. Grant believed that onions prevented <u>dysentery</u> and other illnesses. During the Civil War, he sent a message to the War Department refusing to move his army unless they had onions. A day later, the government sent him three trainloads of onions.

3. <u>dysentery</u> means:     ○ a. bad breath
   ○ b. a type of illness   ○ c. mood swing

Shortly after the Civil War began, Abraham Lincoln asked Robert E. Lee to take command of the Union Army. Lee refused. He later became supreme commander of the <u>Confederate</u> Army.

4. <u>Confederate</u> means:   ○ a. British army
   ○ b. Northern army   ○ c. Southern army

General Stonewall Jackson is buried in two places. His left arm was <u>amputated</u> after the battle of Chancellorsville and buried on a nearby farm. When he died a week later, Jackson was buried in Lexington, Virginia.

5. <u>amputated</u> means:
   ○ a. very loud      ○ b. shot        ○ c. cut off

Name: _____ Date: _____

# Money Matters

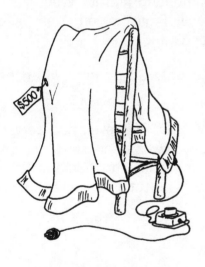

**Directions:** Use reference sources to answer the questions.

The first electric blankets invented in 1912 sometimes caused electrical shocks and even caught on fire. By the 1920s, a safer model was available, but it cost $500.

1. About how much does an electric blanket cost today?

_____

2. What reference source did you use to find the answer?

_____

People complained when they first had to pay federal tax on gasoline in 1932. How much tax did they pay? A penny per gallon!

3. How much tax do we pay per gallon of gas today?

_____

4. What reference source did you use to find the answer?

_____

On February 26, 1907, members of the House and Senate raised their own pay to $7,500. Cabinet members and the vice president earned $12,000 a year.

5. How much does a senator earn today?

_____

6. What reference source did you use to find the answer? _____

In 1920, the average American worker earned $1,500 a year and worked 52 hours a week.

7. What is minimum wage today? _____

8. Use a calculator. Multiply minimum wage times 40. How much would a person earn per week at minimum wage? _____

9. How much would a person earn per year at minimum wage? Multiply the answer to #8 times 52. _____

Name: _____ Date: _____

# President Leslie King?

To **compare** two people means to look for ways in which they are alike.

To **contrast** means to list ways in which they are different.

**William Taft**

★ William Taft, the heaviest man ever to become president, weighed between 300 and 350 pounds. One day, he got completely stuck in the White House bathtub. He ordered a new tub large enough for four people.

★ Gerald Rudolph Ford wasn't the name his parents gave him at birth. They named him Leslie Lynch King, Jr. They divorced when he was two years old. After his mother remarried, her second husband, Gerald R. Ford, adopted him and changed his name.

★ William Henry Harrison served the shortest term. He caught pneumonia on the day he became president and died a month later.

★ His real name was Hiram Ulysses Grant. The congressman who recommended him for West Point submitted his name incorrectly. From then on, Grant used the name Ulysses Simpson Grant instead.

★ James Madison weighed only 98 pounds when he became president.

★ No president before Franklin D. Roosevelt had served more than two terms. Roosevelt was elected as president four times. He died before completing his last term. After his death, a change in the Constitution limited future presidents to two terms.

**Directions:** Answer the following questions about the facts above.

1. How were Taft and Madison different? _____

_____

2. How were Ford and Grant alike? _____

_____

3. How were William Henry Harrison and Franklin Roosevelt different? _____

_____

_____

Name: _____ Date: _____

# Please Pass the Popcorn

**Sequencing** means to arrange events in order from first to last, or earliest to latest.

**Directions:** Read about the history of popcorn. Number the paragraphs in sequential order.

_____ **A.**   Some reports claim that Native Americans brought popcorn to the first Thanksgiving in 1621.

_____ **B.**   Then someone invented a wire basket to hold the kernels over an open fire. This kept the popcorn from jumping all over.

_____ **C.**   People have enjoyed popcorn for thousands of years.

_____ **D.**   By heating popcorn, the small amount of moisture inside each kernel produces steam. Pressure from the steam inside the popcorn causes the outside to burst open.

_____ **E.**   Today, many people prefer microwave popcorn.

_____ **F.**   Finally, popping corn in a closed kettle in oil became the standard method for preparing this treat.

_____ **G.**   At first, people cooked popcorn over glowing coals; however, that didn't work very well. Most of it burned. They tried putting popcorn on top of stones on a hot fire. Fewer kernels burned, but there was another problem. People had to chase the exploding popcorn!

_____ **H.**   Most types of corn look similar, but only one type actually pops. What makes it pop? Believe it or not—water!

Name: _____ Date: _____

# More Money Matters

**Directions:** Use reference sources to complete the following activities.

| **1927 Toy Prices:** | **Today's Toy Prices:** |
|---|---|
| Flying Arrow Sled: $1.39 | _____ |
| Teddy Bear: $1.00 to $2.50 | _____ |
| Board Game: 39 cents | _____ |
| Tinker Toys: 63 cents | _____ |
| Small Erector Set: $1.00 | _____ |

Housewives in Illinois protested the high prices of groceries in November, 1837. Eggs cost 6 cents per dozen; butter, 8 cents per pound; beef, 3 cents per pound; and coffee, 20 cents per pound!

What is the cost today for these items?

one dozen eggs: _____

one pound of butter: _____

one pound of hamburger: _____

one pound of coffee: _____

In 1930, a six-ounce bottle of Coca-Cola™ cost five cents.

How much does a 12-ounce can of Coca-Cola™ cost today?

_____

Name: _____ Date: _____

# Bats in Your Belfry?

**Synonyms** are words that mean the same or nearly the same. *Unique* and *different* are synonyms. A **thesaurus** lists synonyms for words.

**Directions:** Use a thesaurus. Write synonyms for the underlined words.

Belfries were first <u>designed</u> in the Middle Ages for <u>defense</u>. Great areas of the countryside could be <u>observed</u> from this high <u>vantage</u> point. The first belfries were movable wooden towers used in warfare. Later, they came to mean bell towers and became common on Christian churches.

1. designed: _____

   _____

2. defense: _____

   _____

3. observed: _____

   _____

4. vantage: _____

   _____

The ancient Egyptians believed that cats were <u>sacred</u>. They were also very useful for <u>eliminating</u> snakes, rats, and mice.

5. sacred: _____

6. eliminating: _____

Bertha Dlugi wanted to let her pet bird fly freely around her <u>abode</u>, but she didn't want the messy <u>consequences</u>. To solve the problem, she designed an <u>innovative</u> product and <u>obtained</u> a patent in 1956 for her invention: a bird diaper.

7. abode: _____

8. consequences: _____

9. innovative: _____

10. obtained: _____

Name: _____  Date: _____

# How Does Velcro™ Work?

The **main idea** is the most important point made in an article or story.

In 1948, a Swiss engineer, Georges de Mestral, noticed how burrs stuck to his clothing and to his dog as they walked through the woods.

He decided to look at the burrs under his microscope to see what made them stick. He discovered tiny hooks on the ends of the burrs.

These hooks caught onto anything with a loop, like clothing, animal fur, or even human hair, so de Mestral decided to copy nature. It took him several years to get the loops and hooks just right.

He named his invention Velcro™. The word comes from "vel" (for velvet) and "cro" from the French word *crochet* (meaning hook).

Many everyday items like clothes, backpacks, watchbands, toys, and shoes use Velcro™ fasteners. Astronauts use Velcro™ to hold trays, equipment, and even themselves in place in zero gravity.

You might find Velcro™ in nuclear power plants and even army tanks. It's useful for holding flashlights and tools to the walls.

Next time you pick burrs off your clothing or your dog, remember how nature provided the idea for Velcro™.

**Directions:** Answer the following questions about the story above.

1. In your own words, what is the main idea of this article?

   _____

   _____

   _____

2. Briefly explain how Velcro™ works. _____

   _____

3. List three items you own that close with Velcro™. _____

   _____

Name: _____ Date: _____

# Women in the News

A **newspaper headline** is a summary of the most important point in an article. Headlines should be brief, to the point, and grab the reader's attention.

**Annie Oakley**

**Directions:** Write a headline using six words or less for each news item.

1. _____

_____

Annie Oakley broke every sharpshooting record in 1922 at the Pinehurst Gun Club in North Carolina by hitting 98 out of 100 targets.

2. _____

_____

Miriam Ferguson became the first woman elected governor of Texas in 1924. Nicknamed "Ma" Ferguson, banners sported the slogan "Me for Ma."

3. _____

_____

The National Woman Suffrage Association nominated Victoria Claflin Woodhull for President of the United States in 1872.

4. _____

_____

Carry Nation, one of the leaders of the Women's Christian Temperance Union, held prayer meetings and preached against the evils of liquor. Waving a sharp hatchet, she marched into saloons, smashing bottles and furniture. She was often arrested for destroying property. She made public speeches and sold souvenir hatchets to help pay her court costs and fines.

5. _____

Fannie Farmer opened her famous cooking school in 1902. She wanted to make cooking a more scientific process. Many women used recipes that called for a "pinch" of salt, a "handful" of flour, and a "dash" of cinnamon. She adopted standard measurements for cooking and became known as the "Mother of Level Measurement."

Name: _____ Date: _____

# Wooden Bikes?

To learn more about a topic, you can use an **Internet search engine**. A search engine helps you find websites on specific topics.

**Key words** are words or phrases related to a specific topic.

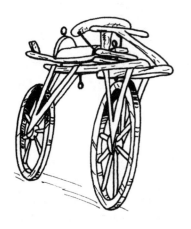

**To use an Internet search engine:**

✔ First type in a key word or phrase. Then click on "GO" or press the "ENTER" key.

✔ If the key word or phrase is too broad, you may get thousands of possible sites. If it is too specific, you may find very few related sites.

The earliest bicycles were made entirely of wood, including the wheels! They had no pedals. To ride, people pushed with their feet along the ground.

Riders couldn't steer the bikes because the front wheel didn't turn from side to side. No problem—as long as you wanted to go straight. Unfortunately, if you wanted to turn, you had to stop, pick up the bike, and point it in a new direction!

1. Use a search engine to complete the activity below. Type in the words given. List the number of sites you found.

| Key word or phrase | Number of sites found |
|---|---|
| transportation | _____ |
| bicycles | _____ |
| antique bicycles | _____ |
| history of bicycles | _____ |
| wooden bicycles | _____ |

2. Use a search engine to find out more about how bicycles have changed since those first early models.

3. List the addresses of two useful websites you found. _____

_____

4. Print illustrations showing at least four very different bicycle designs.

Name: _____  Date: _____

# What's Up, Doc?

**Antonyms** are words that mean the opposite. *Large* and *small* are antonyms. Use a dictionary or some thesauruses to find antonyms.

**Directions:** For each fact below, write antonyms for the underlined words. Use a dictionary or thesaurus if you need help.

1. The <u>youngest</u> Pony Express rider, Bronco Charlie Miller, lived to the age of 105.

   _____

2. When the Korean War <u>began</u>, he tried to enlist, but was turned down. He was 92 years old at the time.

   _____

3. The first Bugs Bunny cartoon <u>appeared</u> in 1940.

   _____

4. Mel Blanc, the man who made the voice of Bugs Bunny <u>famous</u>, had an allergy to carrots.

   _____

5. When he had to make munching carrot sounds, he chewed the carrot, then <u>quickly</u> spit it out.

   _____

6. During leap years when February has 29 days, an old custom <u>allowed</u> women to ask men to marry them.

   _____

7. At one time in France and Scotland, if a man <u>refused</u>, he had to pay a fine.

   _____

8. Congress passed a law ending child <u>labor</u> in 1916. _____

9. In some states, 12-year-old children <u>worked</u> 14 hours a day in mines and factories.

   _____

10. The new law <u>banned</u> children under 16 from working in mines and quarries.

   _____

Name: _____  Date: _____

# Wedding Superstitions

**Superstitions** are beliefs about good and bad luck that many people accept as true.

Here are some superstitions about weddings:

❀ When a chicken comes into the house with a piece of straw in its beak and lays it down, there will be a wedding soon.

❀ Long ago, people in England considered it good luck if you saw a wolf, spider, or toad on your wedding day. Seeing a dog, cat, rabbit, or lizard brought bad luck.

❀ A bride will have good luck if a cat sneezes in front of her on the day before her wedding.

❀ You will shed a tear for each raindrop that falls on your wedding day.

❀ If it snows on your wedding day, you will get a dollar for every flake that falls on you.

❀ Seeing a lamb or dove on the way to church is a sign of good luck, but beware if a pig crosses your path on the way to your wedding!

❀ People today still believe a bride should wear "something old, something new, something borrowed, and something blue" on her wedding day for good luck.

❀ Feed a cat out of an old shoe, and your wedding day will be a happy one.

**Directions:** Circle "T" for true or "F" for false.

1. T   F   People believed that rain on your wedding day meant bad luck.

2. T   F   People thought snow on your wedding day meant bad luck.

3. T   F   They considered it good luck if a pig crossed your path on the way to your wedding.

4. T   F   A cat sneezing before a wedding meant good luck.

5. T   F   People thought seeing a wolf, spider, or toad on your wedding day brought good luck.

Name: _____ Date: _____

# Seeing the Elephant

"I have seen the elephant" is an idiom. This saying came from a story about a farmer who heard the circus was coming to town. Since he had never seen an elephant, he was very excited. He loaded his wagon with vegetables. This would be his big chance. He could see an elephant and make money selling his vegetables as well.

On the way to town, he met the circus parade, led by an elephant. The sight thrilled the farmer but scared his horses. They bolted, overturned the wagon, and ruined the vegetables.

"I don't give a hang," said the farmer, "for I have seen the elephant."

Thousands of people went to California after the discovery of gold in 1848. The journey was long and dangerous. People who set out for California said they were "going to see the elephant."

People who went part of the way but turned back said they had seen "the elephant's tracks" or "the tail of the elephant."

Only those who arrived in California could claim they had "seen the elephant."

**Directions:** Answer the following questions.

1. "I have seen the elephant" is an idiom. What do you think it means?

_____

_____

_____

2. What would "seeing the elephant" be for you?

_____

_____

_____

Name: _____ Date: _____

# Famous Quotes

A **quotation** is the exact words written or spoken by someone. Quotation marks show when the person's words begin and end. Words like *he said* and *she replied* are not part of the quotation.

**Directions:** Underline the quotations in each paragraph.

1.  Buffalo Bill Cody had little formal education. When he wrote his life story, the publisher complained about Cody's punctuation. "Life is too short to make big letters where small ones will do," replied Cody. "And as for punctuation, if my readers don't know enough to take their breath without those little marks, they'll have to lose it, that's all."

2.  President Grover Cleveland wrote an article for the *Ladies Home Journal* published in 1905. He opposed women's right to vote. The former president said, "We all know ... sensible and responsible women do not want to vote."

3.  Martha Truman gave this advice to her son, President Harry S Truman: "... the most important sense a person has is common sense," she told him, "and Harry, you've got more than your share of that. Just use it right, and it will take you a long way."

4.  Abe Lincoln loved to read. "The things I want to know are in books," he said. "My best friend is the man who'll give me a book I haven't read."

5.  Use a reference source to find a quotation you like. Write the quotation, who said it, and the name of the source used.

    _____

    _____

    _____

    _____

**Buffalo Bill Cody**

Name: _____ Date: _____

# The Invention Nobody Wanted

The **main idea** is the most important point made in a story or article. **Details** are points of lesser importance.

In 1893, Whitcomb Judson, a mechanical engineer from Chicago, received a patent for his new invention. He called it a hookless fastener. We know this invention by its modern name: the zipper.

He had two major problems with his invention. It didn't work, and no one wanted it.

Judson displayed his invention at the 1893 Chicago World's Fair. How many did he sell to the 20 million visitors? Twenty—all to the U. S. Postal Service to close their mailbags.

In 1913, Gideon Sundback produced a better model. The U.S. Army ordered zippers for clothing and equipment during World War I.

Unfortunately, these zippers had problems too. They often rusted after washing and couldn't be opened again. Besides that, people didn't know how to work them. (Each zipper came with directions.) Worst of all, no one wanted to buy them.

Then along came B.F. Goodrich with an order for 150,000 zippers in 1923. He wanted hookless fasteners for his new product—rubber galoshes. He liked the z-z-z-zip sound they made and called them zippers.

Once the problems were solved and people learned how to use them, zippers became very popular.

**Directions:** Check details in the article to answer the questions.

1. Who invented the first zipper? _____

2. What were zippers called at first? _____

3. Who renamed them zippers? _____

4. What were two problems with early zippers? _____

_____

5. In your own words, write the main idea of the article.

_____

_____

Name: _____ Date: _____

# Ten O'Clock and All Is Well

Newspapers, news magazines, radio, television, and the **Internet** provide people with news about events.

The town crier held an important position in England and the early American colonies. He acted as a "walking newspaper." The town crier walked around the city, stopping at busy corners to announce town meetings, the time of day, and news of interest.

**Directions:** Complete the following activities.

Today, you have many other ways to learn about what's going on. You can look at a clock or watch to know what time it is.

1. How else can you find out what time it is?

_____

_____

You don't rely on the town crier for news anymore, either. You can read newspapers and magazines, listen to the radio, watch television, or check the Internet.

2. Name a newspaper that provides news about where you live.

_____

You can watch live news from around the world as it happens on TV.

3. Watch a national news show on TV for 20 to 30 minutes. List five major news items you learned about.

_____

_____

You can connect to the Internet and read about news events, past or present. Some Internet sites offer news on special topics, like sports, science, or weather.

4. Write the Internet address of a news website. _____

5. How is a television news announcer similar to a town crier?

_____

_____

Name: _____     Date: _____

# Around the World

An **atlas** contains maps and information about places.

A **globe** is a three-dimensional map of Earth.

**Directions:** Use a globe or atlas to find the answers.

The American Colonization Society was founded in Liberia in 1822 as a refuge for freed slaves.

1. What continent would you be on if you went to Liberia?

_____

Buses in large cities sometimes get very crowded. In London, some buses called "double-deckers" are two stories high.

2. London is the capital of what country?

_____

Buses in Haiti may get so full that people ride on the roof. They call their buses "tap-taps," because people riding on top must tap on the roof to let the driver know when they want to get off.

3. What is the name of the body of water around Haiti?

_____

*Yes or No?* In most places in the world, shaking your head up and down means "yes." Not in Bulgaria and Sri Lanka, however. In those two countries, it means "no." To show they mean "yes," people shake their heads back and forth.

4. Is Sri Lanka in Australia, Africa, Asia, or South America?

_____

5. Name three countries that share a border with Bulgaria.

_____

_____

Name: _____ Date: _____

# Did You Know?

Homophones are words that sound the same. They have different meanings and are not spelled the same. *Sale* and *sail* are homophones.

**Directions:** Circle the correct words. Use a dictionary if you need help.

1. The words September, October, November, and December come from the Latin words ( four, for ) seven, ( ate, eight ), nine, and ten. March was the first month ( in, inn ) the old Roman calendar, ( so, sew ) September was the seventh month, October the eighth, etc.

2. The ancient Egyptians did ( knot, not ) ( know, no ) about fruits like lemons, oranges, bananas, ( pairs, pears ), peaches, and cherries.

3. The people of France presented the 152-foot ( high, hi ) Statue of Liberty ( to, too, two ) the United States ( in, inn ) 1886. She ( weighs, ways ) 225 tons. The statue became a ( symbol, cymbal ) of freedom ( four, for ) immigrants coming ( to, too, two ) the United States.

4. Every year, Santa Claus receives about 15,000 ( peaces, pieces ) of ( mail, male ) at the North Pole—that's North Pole, Arkansas 99705.

5. ( In, Inn ) 1905, people ( in, inn ) the U.S. bought Mrs. Winslow's Soothing Syrup ( to, too, two ) ease babies' teething ( pain, pane ). The relief was provided ( buy, by, bye ) a secret ingredient—morphine.

6. Early electric toasters had ( know, no ) controls ( or, ore, oar ) covers. All of the wires and coils were exposed. They were dangerous ( to, too, two ) use but much more convenient than lighting a fire just ( to, too, two ) toast a ( peace, piece) of ( bred, bread ) ( or, oar, ore ) ( to, too, two).

Name: _____    Date: _____

# Let's Play Monopoly™

To learn more about a topic, you can use an **Internet search engine**. A search engine helps you find websites on specific topics.

**Key words** are words or phrases related to a specific topic.

**To use an Internet search engine:**

✔ First type in a key word or phrase. Then click on "GO" or press the "ENTER" key.

✔ If the key word or phrase is too broad, you may get thousands of possible sites. If it is too specific, you may find very few related sites.

**Directions:** Use an Internet search engine to find the answers to these weird, but true questions.

The word *January* comes from the name of a Roman god with two faces. This allowed him to look backwards into the old year and forward into the new one at the same time.

1.  What was his name? _____

    What key word(s) did you use to find the answer?

    _____

In 1893, the view from Pike's Peak inspired this woman to write a poem that became the song, "America, the Beautiful."

2.  What was her name? _____

    What key word(s) did you use to find the answer? _____

The largest tree on Earth, a 274.9-foot-tall giant sequoia, grows in Sequoia National Park, California. It measures more than 83 feet around its trunk.

3.  What is the name of this tree? _____

    What key word(s) did you use to find the answer? _____

An unemployed salesman invented Monopoly™ in 1932. He thought people might like a game that involved wheeling and dealing for large amounts of cash. Parker Brothers thought the game was too dull and difficult. The inventor borrowed money to make 5,000 games by hand. When they sold quickly, Parker Brothers reconsidered. The unemployed salesman became a millionaire.

4.  Who invented the game of Monopoly™? _____

    What key word(s) did you use to find the answer? _____

33

Name: _____ Date: _____

# Please Pass the Fish Guts Sauce

The **main idea** is the most important point made in a story or article. **Details** are points of lesser importance.

What do fishguts, walnuts, mushrooms, and oysters have in common? All were ingredients used in making ketchup.

Some sources claim the word came from a Chinese sauce called *ke tsiap*. Made from fish guts, it was probably more like soy sauce than modern-day ketchup.

English sailors visiting China in the late 1600s tried it. They found it helped improve the taste of the dried meat they ate aboard ship on long voyages.

In England, the idea of a sauce made from fish guts didn't appeal to many. However, the idea of a flavorful sauce did have potential. People began combining ingredients like mushrooms, walnuts, oysters, and vinegar to make their own version of ketchup.

The idea of ketchup eventually reached the New World. Here too the ingredients varied. Finally, someone came up with a recipe for a tomato-based sauce, and it caught on. One version, known as Dr. Miles' Compound Extract of Tomato, was sold as a patent medicine in the United States in the 1830s.

In 1876, Henry Heinz began bottling and selling ketchup. At that time, tomato ketchup was thin and runny. When people poured it, too much came out too fast. To fix that problem, ketchup makers began using bottles with narrow necks. That helped to slow the flow. The ketchup we enjoy today is much thicker, but the narrow-necked bottles have remained.

**Directions:** Check details in the article to answer the questions.

1. Where did the word *ketchup* come from? _____

2. When did English sailors first try the original form of ketchup? _____

3. What ingredients did people in England use to make ketchup? _____

_____

Compare the ingredients in two different brands of ketchup:

**Brand 1:** _____        **Brand 2:** _____

_____        _____

_____        _____

Name: _____ Date: _____

# The *Turtle* Goes to War

A **dictionary** gives the meanings and pronunciation of words. Some dictionaries list the parts of speech and origins of words.

**Directions:** Use a dictionary to write short definitions for the underlined words.

Today's submarines are large compared to the one <u>designed</u> by David Bushnell during the Revolutionary War. Called the *Turtle,* it measured only seven and a half feet long and six feet wide.

1. designed: _____

_____

Basically egg-shaped, the *Turtle* was <u>constructed</u> of oak and <u>banded</u> with iron. Riding in it must have seemed like being underwater in a barrel.

2. constructed: _____

_____

3. banded: _____

_____

The *Turtle* could dive, move underwater, and <u>surface</u>. The colonists planned to use it against British ships blocking New York Harbor in 1776.

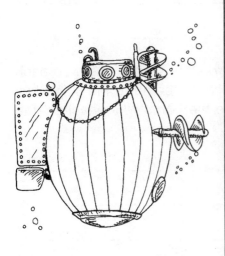

4. surface (verb): _____

Besides being very small, the *Turtle* had other problems. To move it under water, the operator had to <u>vigorously</u> <u>crank</u> a hand-turned <u>propeller</u>.

5. vigorously: _____

6. crank (verb): _____

7. propeller: _____

Name: _____  Date: _____

# The *Turtle* Goes to War (cont.)

Air supply on the *Turtle* was also a problem—it had none. The <u>operator</u> had to bring it to the <u>surface</u> every 30 minutes—or <u>suffocate</u>.

8.  operator: _____

9.  surface (noun): _____

10. suffocate: _____

To <u>descend</u>, the operator opened a valve to admit seawater into a <u>ballast</u> tank. To <u>ascend</u>, he emptied the tank with a hand pump.

11. descend: _____

12. ballast: _____

13. ascend: _____

The sub carried a gunpowder bomb with a time <u>fuse</u>. The *Turtle's* <u>mission</u> was to approach an enemy ship under water. The operator planned to <u>attach</u> the bomb to the ship's hull using a screw <u>device</u> operated from within the craft. Once the bomb was attached, the *Turtle* needed to escape before the bomb exploded.

14. fuse (noun): _____

15. mission: _____

16. attach: _____

17. device: _____

Sergeant Ezra Lee of the Continental Army made the one and only <u>attempt</u> to use the *Turtle* in battle. Lee floated the *Turtle* against the hull of the British <u>flagship</u> HMS *Eagle,* but he could not attach the bomb because the ship's <u>hull</u> was copperplated. Lee and the *Turtle* escaped, but that was the end of the war for the *Turtle*.

18. attempt: _____

19. flagship: _____

20. hull: _____

Name: _____ Date: _____

# Workers Earn $5 a Day!

An **adjective** is a word that describes a noun. *Fast, happy,* and *cold* are adjectives.

**Directions:** Circle all of the adjectives.

1. Henry Ford built his first car in 1896.

2. By 1908, the Ford Motor Company produced a simple, reliable car called the Model T.

3. Nicknamed the Tin Lizzie, its 20-horsepower engine allowed drivers to reach a top speed of 40 miles per hour.

4. For $850, people could buy a Tin Lizzie "in any color, as long as it was black!"

5. In 1913, Henry Ford introduced the assembly line idea to car manufacturing.

6. As conveyor belts moved the vehicles along, workers added parts.

7. Not only could they make more cars this way, but the cost of each car was also lower.

8. The 1913 model cost only $260.

9. Workers earned $5 a day—a great amount of money for a factory worker at that time.

10. Henry Ford took another innovative step in auto making in 1925.

11. For the first time, people had a choice of colors: gunmetal blue, highland green, phoenix brown, fawn gray, and of course, black.

12. In 1927, the Ford Motor Company replaced the Model T with the more modern Model A, which sold for $395.

13. Employees of the Ford Motor Company received a fantastic raise on December 3, 1928, when their pay went up to $7 per day.

**Model T**

**Model A**

Name: _____ Date: _____

# Never on Sunday

You can sometimes understand the meaning of a word you don't know by using context clues.

**Context clues** are other words in the sentence or paragraph that help explain the meaning of the word.

**Directions:** Use context clues to select the meaning for the underlined words.

In the 1880s, some states made it <u>illegal</u> to sell ice cream sodas on Sunday. (An ice cream soda included a scoop of ice cream, <u>carbonated water</u>, and flavored syrup.)

Soda fountain owners found a way to get around the law by <u>eliminating</u> the bubbly carbonated water. They served a <u>scoop</u> of ice cream with syrup and a cherry on top. This became known as a "Sunday soda." We now call it an ice cream sundae.

1. <u>Illegal</u> means:   ○ a.  not healthy
   ○ b.  against the law          ○ c.  fun

2. <u>Eliminating</u> means: ○ a.  adding   ○ b.  taking out
   ○ c.  against the law

3. <u>Scoop</u> means:   ○ a.  a spoonful
   ○ b.  to make ice cream          ○ c.  a shovel

4. From the context clues, what do you think *carbonated water* means?

_____

The ice cream cone was invented at the 1904 St. Louis World's Fair, when a man selling ice cream ran out of paper dishes. He bought a waffle from another <u>vendor</u>, rolled it into a cone shape, and stuck a scoop of ice cream on top. The official name of this tasty <u>invention</u> was the "World's Fair Cornucopia."

5. <u>Vendor</u> means:      ○ a.  a person who makes waffles
   ○ b.  a person who sells something      ○ c.  a visitor at the fair

6. <u>Invention</u> means:   ○ a.  an invitation   ○ b.  a cone-shaped item
   ○ c.  something new

In July 1988, the Palm Dairies, Ltd., in Canada made an ice cream <u>sundae</u> that weighed over 54,914 pounds. This delicious dessert included more than 44,689 pounds of ice cream, 9,688 pounds of syrup, and 537 pounds of toppings.

7. <u>Sundae</u> means:      ○ a.  the first day of the week   ○ b.  a city in New York
   ○ c.  an ice cream treat

Name: _____ Date: _____

# Then and Now

To **compare** two people means to look for ways in which they are alike.

To **contrast** means to list ways in which they are different.

**Susan B. Anthony**

**Directions:** Read the statements. Write a sentence that shows the ways in which things have changed—or the ways in which they have stayed the same. Use your own paper if you need more room.

1. **THEN:** By 1800, there were only about 50 libraries in the United States. Altogether, the libraries contained about 80,000 books. Most of the early libraries required people to pay dues or fees to borrow books.

   **NOW:** _____

   _____

   _____

2. **THEN:** Susan B. Anthony was arrested on November 6, 1875, for trying to vote.

   **NOW:** _____

   _____

3. **THEN:** In 1900, only 2% of Americans owned a telephone. No one owned a radio or a television.

   **NOW:** _____

   _____

4. **THEN:** In 1900, there were only 150 miles of paved roads in the whole country.

   **NOW:** _____

5. **THEN:** In 1919, only about one-third of American homes had electricity.

   **NOW:** _____

6. **THEN:** In 1939, you could have gone to the movies and watched a cartoon, a newsreel, and one of the all-time hits, *The Wizard of Oz,* and also bought two large candy bars—all for only a quarter!

   **NOW:** _____

Name: _____ Date: _____

# What's in an Index?

An **index** is an alphabetical listing of words and phrases for major topics in a book or set of books. Indexes are usually found in non-fiction books.

**Directions:** Use the index of an encyclopedia to answer the first three questions.

1. On what page(s) would you find information about the North Pole? _____

2. On what page(s) would you find information about bat sharks? _____

3. What are the titles of articles that include information about bubble gum?

   _____

   _____

**Directions:** Use the index of an atlas to answer the next three questions.

4. If you'd like to ride a trolley car, take a trip to San Francisco. On what page would you find a map that showed the location of this city of hills?

   _____

5. Chicago has been nicknamed the "Windy City." On what page would you find a map of this city?

   _____

6. Would you like to go spelunking? You can explore caves at Mammoth Cave National Park. On what page would you find a map that shows the location of this site?

   _____

**Directions:** Use what you learned about indexes to answer these questions on your own paper.

7. How is an index different from a dictionary?

8. How is the table of contents of a book different from an index?

9. Why do you think fiction books do not have indexes?

Name: _____ Date: _____

# Would You Like to Buy an Edsel?

**Directions:** Use a thesaurus. Write synonyms for the underlined words.

After three years of underlined research, Ford introduced the Edsel in 1957. Instead of being America's dream car, the Edsel turned out to be Ford's nightmare. People wouldn't purchase them. Thieves wouldn't even steal them. During the three years Ford manufactured this unpopular car, only one Edsel was reported stolen.

1. research: _____

2. purchase: _____

3. manufactured: _____

Seventeen-year-old Belle Boyd became a notorious spy for the South during the Civil War. Although captured by Lieutenant Samuel Haringe near the conclusion of the war, she didn't go to prison. Instead, he married her, resigned from the U.S. Navy, and enlisted with the Confederates.

**Edsel**

4. notorious: _____

5. captured: _____

6. resigned: _____

7. enlisted: _____

Meeting a school of dolphins at sea was considered a good omen by Roman sailors.

8. omen: _____

In 1830, Sylvester Graham developed a product made of coarsely ground whole wheat flour. He called it Graham bread. We call it a graham cracker. Graham also believed that people should bathe at least three times a week, and get fresh air and daily exercise. His ideas were contrary to what most people, even doctors, believed.

9. developed: _____

10. coarsely: _____

11. contrary: _____

Name: _____ Date: _____

# When Is the Mall Like a Boat?

**Homophones** are words that sound the same. They have different meanings and are not spelled the same. *Hail* and *hale* are homophones. **Puns** are jokes that often use homophones.

**Directions:** Write the correct homophone for the underlined word in each pun.

1.  **Question:** What happens to illegally parked frogs?
    **Answer:** They get <u>toad</u> away.

    _____

2.  **Question:** When is the mall like a boat?
    **Answer:** When it has <u>sales</u>

    _____

3.  **Question:** What part of a horse is the most important?
    **Answer:** The <u>mane</u> part

    _____

4.  **Question:** Why couldn't the pony talk?
    **Answer:** He was a little <u>horse</u>.

    _____

5.  **Question:** What kind of tree is dressed warmly?
    **Answer:** A <u>fir</u> tree

    _____

6.  **Question:** Why don't bears wear shoes and socks?
    **Answer:** Because they like to go <u>bear</u> foot.

    _____

7.  **Question:** How was the rock braver than the mountain?
    **Answer:** Because it was a little <u>boulder</u>

    _____

8.  **Question:** What animal do most people have on their heads?
    **Answer:** <u>Hare</u>

    _____

9.  **Question:** What color is the wind?
    **Answer:** <u>Blew</u>

    _____

10. **Question:** Why did the baker stop making doughnuts?
    **Answer:** He got tired of the <u>hole</u> business.

    _____

11. **Question:** What did one penny say to another penny?
    **Answer:** "Together we make <u>cents</u>."

    _____

# Scavenger Hunt

**Reference sources** include books, newspapers, magazines, CDs, and Internet sites. The type of reference source you use depends on your topic. Always use the most recent sources you can find.

**Directions:** Use reference sources to hunt for these answers.

On December 6, 1902, she became the first American woman pictured on a U.S. stamp.

1. What was her name? _____

Alexander Graham Bell sent the first telephone message to his assistant, Mr. Watson.

2. What were his first words? _____

_____

3. When did that call take place? _____

According to legend, the Pied Piper of this German city played his tunes in 1284. When city officials refused to pay him for getting rid of the rats, the piper played another tune. All the children of the town followed him into a hole in a hill, never to be seen again.

4. What was the name of the city? _____

The Soviet Union launched the first satellite to orbit Earth. The craft circled Earth every 95 minutes at almost 2,000 miles per hour until it fell from the sky three months later.

5. What was the name of the satellite? _____

6. In what year was it launched? _____

When this woman began the first troop of Girl Scouts, only 18 girls joined. When she died 15 years later, over 140,000 girls across the nation had become Girl Scouts.

7. Who started the first Girl Scout troop? _____

8. In what city? _____

9. In what year? _____

Not only was she the first woman to swim across the cold, choppy English Channel, but she also did it in record time. It took her 14 hours and 31 minutes—the best time to that date, beating the men's record by two hours.

10. What was her name? _____

11. When did she break the record? _____

# Check It Out!

You can find lots of weird, but true information at your library and on the Internet. Check out these sources.

Bruce Adelson: *Grand Slam Trivia: Secrets, Statistics, and Little-Known Facts about Pro Baseball.*

Bruce Adelson: *Hat Trick Trivia: Secrets, Statistics, and Little-Known Facts about Hockey.*

Bruce Adelson: *Slam Dunk Trivia: Secrets, Statistics, and Little-Known Facts about Basketball.*

Bruce Adelson: *Touchdown Trivia: Secrets, Statistics, and Little-Known Facts about Football.*

Burke Davis: *The Civil War: Strange and Fascinating Facts.*

The Diagram Group: *Funky, Freaky Facts Most People Don't Know.*

*Guiness Book of World Records:* This is an annual publication, so check out the most recent copy you can find.

Stephen J. Lang: *Big Book of American Trivia.*

Carol Marsh: *Gee! Ology: Trivia for Kids.*

Stanley Newman: *10,000 Answers: The Ultimate Trivia Encyclopedia.*

Caroline Sutton: *How Do They Do That?: Wonders of the Modern World Explained.*

Howard Zimmerman: *Ripley's Believe It or Not!: Great and Strange Works of Man.*

**Websites:**

www.coolquiz.com/trivia

www.discoverychannel.com

www.enchantedlearning.com

www.guinessworldrecords.com

http://historychannel.com

New websites appear frequently, and sometimes old ones disappear. You can find more cool trivia and weird, but true information with a search engine.

# Answer Keys

**The Cold Shoulder (page 3)**
1. you; expression, someone; shoulder
2. It; someone; person; respect
3. expression, hundreds; years; England
4. guest; knight; castle; people; him; respect; honor
5. host; meat; drink
6. Others; castle
7. They; water; plate, meat; mutton
8. shoulder; parts; meat
9. Visitors; piece; shoulder
10. you; classmate; someone; game; activity; you; person; disrespect; shoulder

**All Aboard for Teakettle Junction! (page 5–6)**
Teacher check map.

**Rollo, the Red-Nosed Reindeer? (page 8)**
1. author 2. solved
3. decided 4. shiny
5. rescued 6. insisted
7. unique 8. illustrated

**President Fined for Speeding (page 10)**
1. Ulysses S. Grant
2. George Washington, Thomas Jefferson, John Adams
3. John Quincy Adams; White House; Louisa Adams; Potomac River
4. Millard Fillmore; New Hope Academy
5. Harry S Truman; Truman
6. Abe Lincoln
7. President, United States, James Garfield, Latin, Greek

**In the White House (page 11)**
1. installed: put in
2. available: at hand; accessible
3. formal: conventional
4. creative: unique, unusual
5. avoided: stayed away from
6. drafted: selected for military service
7. substitute: something in place of something else

**Where Did Santa Claus Come From? (page 14)**
1. cheeks were like roses,
nose like a cherry
mouth like a bow,
beard as white as the snow.
smoke encircled his head like a wreath
belly shook like a bowlful of jelly

**Up, Up, and Away (page 15)**
1. took, left, landed
2. avoid, landing, forced, throw, thrown
3. made, fly, fly
4. planned, introduce, gathered, watch
5. get, started, got, discovered
6. fixed, took, went, made, get, broke
7. arrived, picked, drove
8. left, fly, landed, found
9. received, claimed, followed

**Generally Speaking (page 16)**
1. a  2. b  3. b  4. c  5. c

**President Leslie King? (page 18)**
1. Taft weighed the most, and Madison weighed the least when president.
2. Both had their names changed before they became president.
3. Harrison served the shortest term, and Roosevelt served the longest term as president.

**Please Pass the Popcorn (page 19)**
A. 2  B. 6  C. 1  D. 4  E. 8  F. 7
G. 5  H. 3

**Wedding Superstitions (page 26)**
1. T  2. F  3. F  4. T  5. T

**Famous Quotes (page 28)**
1. "Life is too short to make big letters where small ones will do,"
"And as for punctuation, if my readers don't know enough to take their breath without those little marks, they'll have to lose it, that's all."
2. "We all know ... sensible and responsible women do not want to vote."
3. "... the most important sense a person has is common sense," "and Harry, you've got more than your share of that. Just use it right, and it will take you a long way."
4. "The things I want to know are in books,"
"My best friend is the man who'll give me a book I haven't read."

**The Invention Nobody Wanted (page 29)**
1. Whitcomb Judson
2. hookless fasteners
3. B.F. Goodrich
4. Any two: They didn't work. They rusted. People didn't know how to use them. No one wanted to buy them.

## Around the World (page 31)
1. Africa
2. England
3. Caribbean Sea
4. Asia
5. Any three: Turkey, Greece, Yugoslavia, Romania, Macedonia

## Did You Know? (page 32)
1. for; eight; in; so
2. not; know; pears
3. high; to; in; weighs; symbol; for; to
4. pieces; mail
5. In; in; to; pain; by
6. no; or; to; to; piece; bread; or; two

## Let's Play Monopoly™ (page 33)
1. Janus
2. Katharine Lee Bates
3. General Sherman
4. Charles Darrow

## Please Pass the Fish Guts Sauce (page 34)
1. the Chinese word *ke tsiap*
2. in the late 1600s
3. mushrooms, walnuts, oysters, and vinegar

## The *Turtle* Goes to War (page 35–36)
1. designed: created
2. constructed: made
3. banded: circled
4. surface: rise to the top of the water
5. vigorously: with great force
6. crank: turn
7. propeller: blades that turn to move something
8. operator: a person who uses a machine
9. surface: top
10. suffocate: run out of air
11. descend: go down
12. ballast: weight used to keep something down
13. ascend: go up
14. fuse: part of a bomb that burns
15. mission: job
16. attach: join
17. device: tool
18. attempt: try
19. flagship: ship that carries the commander of a fleet
20. hull: outer part of a ship

## Workers Earn $5 a Day! (page 37)
1. his; first
2. simple, reliable
3. 20-horsepower; top; 40
4. any; black
5. assembly line; car
6. conveyor
7. more; this; each; lower
8. 1913
9. great; factory; that
10. another; innovative; auto
11. first; gunmetal; highland; phoenix; fawn
12. modern
13. fantastic; their

## Never On Sunday (page 38)
1. b    2. b    3. a
4. water with bubbles
5. b    6. c    7. c

## When Is the Mall Like a Boat? (page 42)
1. towed
2. sails
3. main
4. hoarse
5. fur
6. bare
7. bolder
8. hair
9. blue
10. whole
11. sense

## Scavenger Hunt (page 43)
1. Martha Washington
2. "Mr. Watson, come here. I want you."
3. March 10, 1876
4. Hamelin
5. *Sputnik I*
6. 1957
7. Juliette Low
8. Savannah, Georgia
9. 1912
10. Gertrude Ederle
11. August 6, 1926